Ian Morrison

The Mary Rose:
her wreck and rescue

Lutterworth Press · Guildford · Surrey · England

Some nations are lucky in their maritime heritage. As well as models in museums, they have full-sized ships that have survived from the past, and people of the present day can actually visit vessels involved in exciting parts of their history. The Norwegians have real Viking ships at Oslo; the Americans have the frigate Constitution *from the end of the 18th century; and the Swedes have the great royal ship* Wasa, *built at the start of the 17th century.*

England is particularly fortunate. Among merchant ships there is the Cutty Sark *at Greenwich and the* Great Britain *at Bristol; and at the great naval dockyard of Portsmouth there are historic warships. One is* HMS Victory, *on which Admiral Nelson won the Battle of Trafalgar in 1805. Another is the* Mary Rose. *She dates back to the time of Henry VIII, King of England from 1509 to 1547. Portsmouth is her home port: she was built there in 1509. But she only returned home in 1982, thanks to the efforts of underwater archaeologists. In 1545, during a war with the French, she sank nearby in the Solent, and her remains were preserved in the mud of the sea-bed.*

We are extraordinarily lucky to have inherited a Tudor ship nearly five centuries old, particularly one associated with Henry VIII, who has been described as 'the father of the Royal Navy'.

Mary Rose *marks a key stage in the change-over from the kind of sea warfare that had gone on in the Middle Ages, when warships were thought of as bases for waging land-style battles afloat and were built with high 'castles' fore and aft, to carry soldiers firing at each other. When she was built, experiments were being made in taking to sea cannons big enough to sink ships. This new style of naval warfare was to last right through the centuries to the days of* HMS Victory.

The big heavy cannons with which a Tudor warship was
armed would have rolled her over If they had been
carried in the high forecastle and sterncastle. So
they were kept low down, and gunports – holes through
which they could be fired – were cut close to the water-
line. This brought a new danger because if the ship
heeled over, water might flood in there. Later ships,
like Nelson's *Victory*, had a safer balance between
height and weight, and gunport lids which were better at
keeping out water. Their builders had learnt from the
mistakes that were made at the time of *Mary Rose*, when
the new ideas for arming ships were first being tried out.

Many people think that the coming of William the
Conqueror in 1066 was the last time foreign troops
invaded England, and that the first real threat after
that was the Spanish Armada, in 1588. But in 1545
only Henry VIII's navy stood between England and
a French fleet of 235 ships (a hundred more than the
Armada), carrying 30,000 men. At that time, the
English still ruled parts of France, including Calais,
and Henry had recently captured the port of Boulogne
from his old rival, Francis I, the French king.
Now Francis wanted Boulogne back.

Francis planned to attack Portsmouth, Henry's main base
on the south coast. His invasion fleet included 25
great galleys from the Mediterranean, commanded by
Knights of Malta, some of the best fighting seamen of the
age. Rowed by slaves, the galleys could attack even
when there was no wind. At Portsmouth, Henry had only
60 ships – some of them very small. He probably
crowded every possible man and weapon aboard his main
warships, *Great Harry* and *Mary Rose*. The English would
be fighting on their own doorstep, and the sea was calm
so they may well have overloaded the ships.

5

On Saturday, the 18th of July, 1545, Henry held a council of war aboard the *Great Harry*. She was the flagship, under the command of the Lord Admiral, Viscount Lisle. Henry appointed Sir George Carew to be Vice-Admiral and second-in-command, aboard *Mary Rose*. Musical instruments were carried on the royal ships (some were found in the wreck) and minstrels may well have played to celebrate Sir George's promotion. But though the King was a keen musician, and though the Vice-Admiral's badge of office was a golden whistle hung round his neck, neither man can have felt much like joining in with the music.

The enemy might come into sight at any moment. The English knew that the French had nearly three times as many fighting men in their fleet as were crammed aboard King Henry's ships in Portsmouth. And in the almost windless weather, the Mediterranean galleys, rowed by hundreds of trained oarsmen, could run rings round the heavy English sailing ships and, given half a chance, would riddle them with shot. If the French army was to be prevented from landing, the English navy must avoid being lured into a position where its ships could be destroyed.

It was to be a game of cat and mouse. The French cat
was certainly a very large one, and its galleys gave it
speedy paws with long claws. But the English mouse did
have teeth, and the advantage of knowing its own
mousehole. The waters off Portsmouth are shallow and
unless you know where the deep channels lie, and
understand the currents that run like invisible rivers
along them as the tide ebbs and flows, it is all too easy
to go aground.

The cat must be almost upon them. Sir Peter Carew, the
new Vice-Admiral's brother, swarmed up the rigging of the
mainmast. To Henry's shout, 'What news?', he called that
he could see three or four ships but they looked like
merchantmen. But soon more and more ships were coming
up over the horizon, and he cried out that he could see
a great fleet of men-o'-war. . . . The cat had arrived.

Henry sent his captains to their ships and called for a
long-boat to take him ashore to Southsea Castle, where
he would have a clear view of the whole battle area.

Soon the first paw came reaching into the mousehole. The
French Admiral, D'Annebault, sent forward his galleys.
A breeze blowing off the land let the English ships sail
to meet them. There was the flash and crash of guns.
But instead of going right out into the open sea, where
the French could surround them, the English ships turned
away behind the shallow waters of the Horse Sand.
To get at them there, the French would have had to
find their way along a hidden channel of deep water,
so narrow that only a few of them could come at a time.
If they had done this, they would have been under fire
from Henry's forts on shore. They did not try.
Night was falling, and they had troubles of their own.
The French flagship had sunk.

Mary Rose was not to be the only Admiral's ship sunk
in that war. Even as the French were setting out for
England, their first flagship, the *Carraquon*, had caught
fire and sunk. Admiral D'Annebault had taken over *La
Maistresse* instead, but *she* had bumped on the sea-bed
as she was coming out of port, and though the French
had carried on towards England, she was more badly damaged
than they had realised. Now *La Maistresse* had sprung a
leak, and sunk in the shallow waters off the Isle of Wight.
The French did manage to salvage her, but she was out
of the fight.

Sunday, the 19th of July, dawned bright and calm, and once
again D'Annebault sent the galleys forward as a cat's paw
to fetch the English into the open sea, where his fleet
could destroy them. At first the English ships could only
lie at anchor while the galleys bombarded them, but at
last the tide turned, and the wind got up. The *Great Harry*
weighed anchor and led the main column of the English ships
out against the enemy, while Sir George Carew, aboard *Mary
Rose*, led the left-hand column. He may well have thought
that, like the tide, their luck had turned for the better,
but in fact few men aboard *Mary Rose* had long to live.

11

We are not sure why *Mary Rose* sank. The French thought they had sunk her. After all, if you are firing at an enemy ship, and she suddenly rolls over and sinks, you naturally assume that your cannons have something to do with it – and so they may have done. The English main column, led by the *Great Harry*, was to the right-hand, or 'starboard', side of *Mary Rose*, so her left-hand or 'port' side would have been more exposed to French cannon balls. But most of her port side rotted away during the centuries after she went down, so we cannot tell how successful the French were in damaging her.

Whatever the French thought, the English didn't give them the credit for sinking the ship, though nobody knew for certain how it happened. Some people thought there was trouble among her crew. Sir Peter Carew has left an account telling how she heeled over steeply as soon as her sails were hoisted, and how Sir Gawain Carew sailed close by on his own ship the *Matthew Gonson*, to ask his nephew Sir George on *Mary Rose* what was wrong. The Vice-Admiral shouted back, 'I have the sort of knaves I cannot rule . . .' These were his last words that we know of, before he went down with his ship.

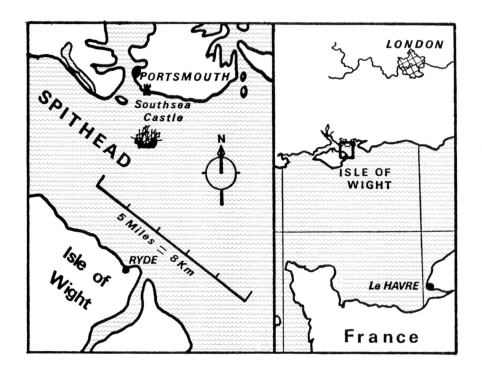

The battle area, where Mary Rose *sank*

Quick action might have saved *Mary Rose*. There were
a hundred expert seamen aboard her. They may have been
hampered by all the archers and soldiers crowded into
the ship, but perhaps they died because of their own pride,
as Sir George's last message suggests. Sir Peter said
that each of those sailors could have been a master of
a ship in his own right, but just because of this they
thought they were above taking orders. As he put it:
'Refusing to do that which they should do . . . contending
in envy, they perished.'

Whatever the parts played by crew trouble and battle
damage, it was the heeling-over that sent *Mary Rose* so
abruptly to the bottom.

Underwater archaeologists have confirmed that her guns were ready for action and her gunports lashed wide open. As soon as she heeled far enough over for the sea to flood in through those new-style gunports, so close to the water-line, the fate of those aboard was sealed.

As hundreds of tons of water surged into the ship, guns broke loose and smashed across the wildly canting decks packed with struggling men. *Mary Rose* went down so violently that her hull drove two or three metres deep into the mud, fifteen metres below the sea's surface.

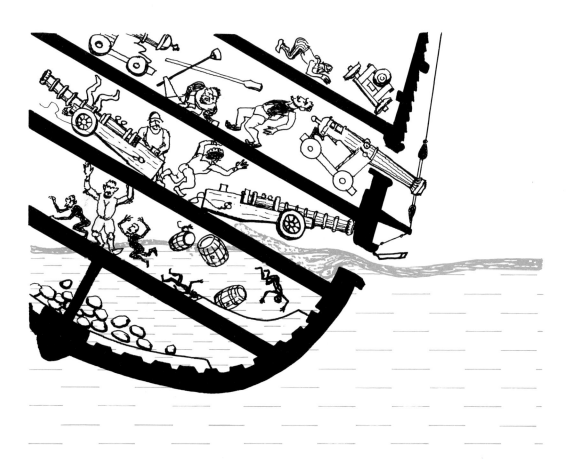

For the men packed below decks, there was no real hope.
They died in the dark. Some of the sick and wounded
drowned as they lay on their mattresses in the hold. Many
who did manage to scramble up towards the daylight must
have been trapped by the nets that had been stretched
above the decks in case the French tried to board *Mary Rose*.
And even those who got clear were still doomed to drown if
they could not get out of their armour in time.

Of perhaps 700 men aboard, only about three dozen were
saved. They were mostly lightly clad servants and sailors.
Some were found clinging to the masts of the sunken ship,
which still showed above the waves.

People on shore heard the last long cry of despair as those aboard 'drowned like rattens'. And though rats are supposed to show an instinct for leaving doomed ships, *Mary Rose* went down so fast that their bones, too, have been found in the wreck.

Lady Mary Carew was watching the battle with King Henry from the ramparts of Southsea Castle. She fainted as she saw her husband's great ship vanish, dragging him down into the Solent with his men. As Henry comforted her, he remarked that he hoped that after this hard beginning, there would follow a better ending . . .

Some of the most touching finds from the wreck were the personal property of the crew, like this manicure set

Eventually there was indeed 'a better ending', for
although the French attacked the Isle of Wight and the
Sussex coast, they did finally give up and sail home
without landing their great invasion army. But at first
nobody knew things would work out so well, and Henry was
keen to see if *Mary Rose* could be raised (after all, the
French had salvaged *La Maistresse*). He gave the job to
Symone de Maryne and Petre de Andreas, experts from
Venice who were visiting England. They decided to try
to lift *Mary Rose* by using two other ships, each as
large as she was. Henry provided the *Sampson* and the
Jesus of Lubeck, and within a fortnight they had them
ready for the first attempt.

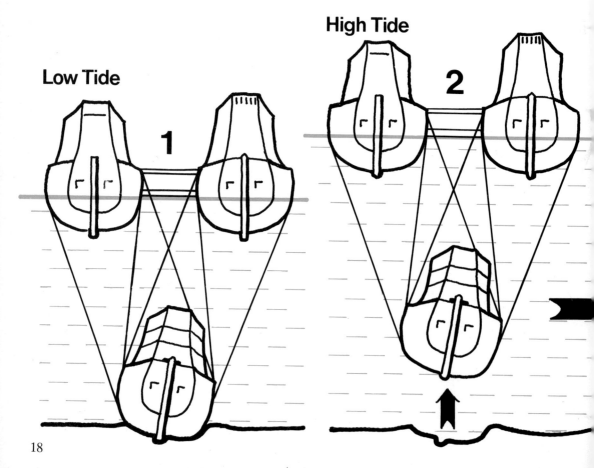

The Venetians planned to tie these two ships firmly to the wrecked warship, tightening the ropes when the tide was low. As the tide came in and the water rose, *Samson* and *Jesus of Lubeck* would float upwards and should raise *Mary Rose* off the sea-bed. They could then tow her between them, hanging in a cradle of ropes, until she grounded again, closer to shore. As the tide ebbed, and the water level fell, the ropes tying the salvage ships to *Mary Rose* would go slack. That meant they could be shortened; the next high tide would lift the ships again, and carry *Mary Rose* into shallower water; and so on until she was so near the shore that she would emerge at low tide, and could be emptied and repaired.

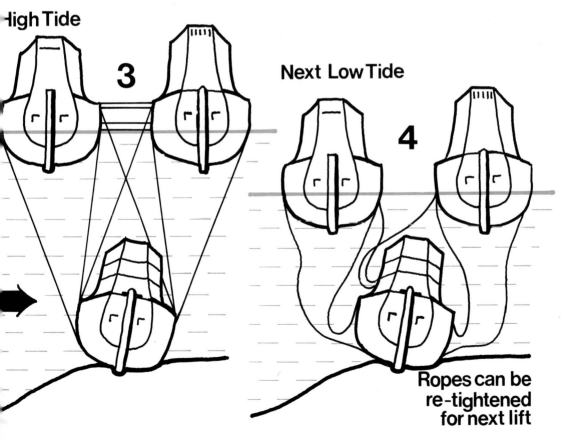

High Tide

3

Next Low Tide

4

Ropes can be re-tightened for next lift

It was a good idea which had already been used to raise other sunken ships, and which has often been used since then. But *Mary Rose* refused to move – probably because she had embedded herself in the mud. She was lying on her side, and to get a clean lift they needed to bring her upright; but without modern diving-gear they could not burrow under the hull and pass cables underneath her. At first they tried to shift her by tying ropes to her masts but the foremast broke and (as archaeologists have discovered) the mainmast was pulled right out of her. The Venetians then tried to drag her towards the shallows on her side – but that did not work either.

16th Century

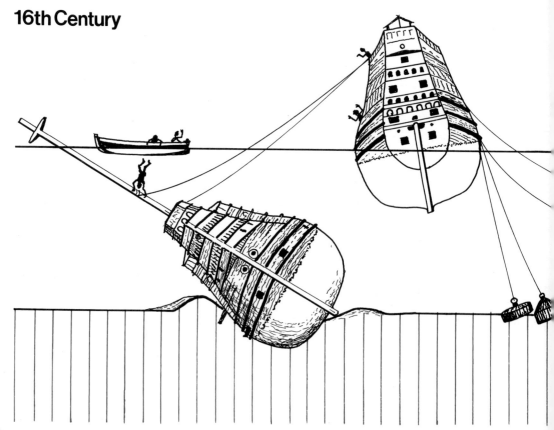

The threat of invasion passed, and with it went the urgency of the attempt to salvage *Mary Rose*. After the next four years, when a few guns were fished up, little more interest was taken in the wreck.

Mud soon filled much of the inside of the hull, sealing off the buried starboard side and preserving the things which modern archaeologists have discovered. But the port side still stuck up from the sea-bed, and as years passed into centuries, its timbers rotted, and were eaten away by gribble and other nibblers and borers, until at last it collapsed. Gravel and shells spread over the wreck, and by the 19th century, *Mary Rose* had literally dropped from view.

17th Century   20th Century

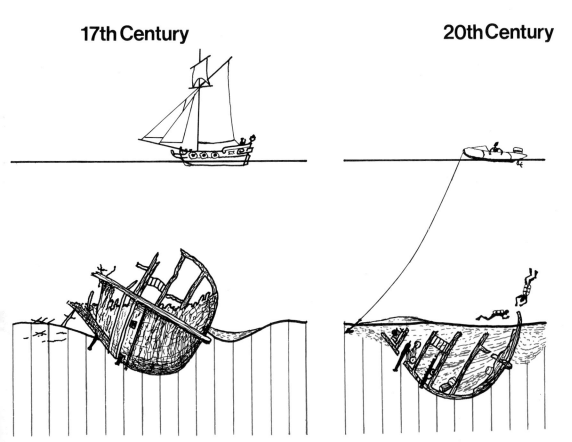

The *Mary Rose* was first rediscovered because of an even greater disaster nearby. In 1782, the 108-gun *Royal George* sank there while she lay at anchor, drowning nine hundred people, among them women and children visiting the crew. Attempts to raise her failed. Half a century later, the Deane family of professional divers started salvaging her cannons.

One day in 1836, a Gosport boat that was fishing near where the Deanes were working snagged her net on the sea-bed. The fishermen's nets had got caught there before, and they suspected that there might be another wreck, perhaps with something worth salvage money. So they asked the Deanes to take a look, offering to share any profits with them. John Deane went down, and found that there was very little showing above the sea-bed. The net had caught on just one blackened timber. But there certainly was a wreck buried there – he found a bronze cannon more than twice as long as he was. When they hauled it to the surface, they found it had trunnions in the shape of lions' heads, and a Tudor Rose over an inscription stating that it had been cast in 1542 for King Henry VIII. . . . *Mary Rose* had been found again.

Over the next four years, the Deanes brought up several bronze and iron guns (some still on their wooden carriages, and still loaded with their cannon balls and gunpowder). They found some of the archers' long-bows, and even recovered pieces of cloth, as well as unbroken bottles and pottery – and human skulls.

Although the Deanes had the objects that they brought up measured and recorded in drawings beautifully coloured in water-colour, they were hardly underwater archaeologists in the best modern sense – they even used explosives to try to get more finds which they could sell.

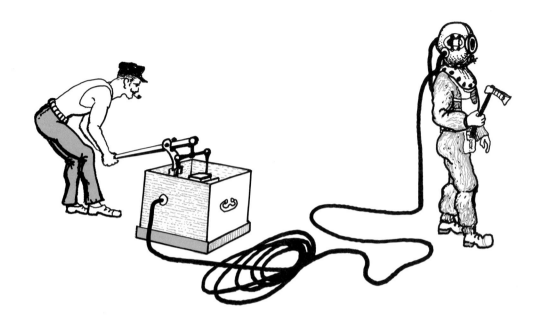

However, modern underwater work of all kinds owes a great
deal to the Deanes, for it was they who developed the first
really practical diving-gear. Strangely, their inspiration
came not from water, but from fire. When he was just
eighteen, John Deane helped save horses from a burning barn.
The farmer had an old pump, but its water-jet was too weak
to deal with the flames, and the choking smoke prevented
anyone from getting into the barn to set the horses free.
John took the helmet off an old suit of armour in the
farmhouse and got the farmer to pump air, not water,
down the hose-pipe. Wearing the helmet with the hose
stuck into it, he found he could breathe despite the smoke,
and he was able to bring out all the horses.

In the years that followed, he and his brother Charles
developed not only breathing-sets for firemen, but the
kind of copper-helmet diving-gear that was to be used in
all the seas of the world for well over a century.

Although the kind of diving-gear that the Deanes had
developed became so widely used, their names were soon
forgotten. And so too was *Mary Rose*, when they ceased
to raise objects from her. Once more the wreck dropped
out of sight, and after the 1840s even its position
was lost.

It was not until the 1960s that interest in *Mary Rose*
revived. By then the invention of the aqualung,
developed by Cousteau, had changed the whole face of diving.

The old-style divers, using the type of gear pioneered
by the Deanes, were tethered by their air-hoses and
weighed down by their lead boots, and could never rove
freely – unlike the new aqualung divers with their
self-contained bottles of compressed air, and their flippers.

Now many people could and did take up diving purely as a
sport. Others found that the aqualung allowed them to
pursue their particular interests into the underwater world.
Diving became possible for properly trained archaeologists
like Margaret Rule and Andrew Fielding (who were to become
directors of the excavation of *Mary Rose*), and for the
hundreds of amateurs who were keen to join in archaeological
projects. Had this not been so, the *Mary Rose* would
probably still be lying unexcavated in the Solent today.

But first she had to be found again. During the 1960s much
of the energy behind the search came from Alexander McKee,
a professional writer with a keen interest in maritime
history, who was also an amateur diver. At that time,
few people believed that really well-preserved wrecks of
any great age could survive outside the special conditions
of the Mediterranean. McKee did not accept this, and he
led many searches in the Solent. But *Mary Rose* escaped him
for several years.

This time there were no lucky reports from fishermen.
Instead the break-through came with the help of scientific
devices which would have delighted those earlier inventors,
John and Charles Deane (though they could hardly have
imagined them, any more than Henry VIII himself might
have done). Professor Harold Edgerton and John Mills
used electronics and ultra-sound to 'see' through the
murky water with side-scan sonar, and to look deep into
the mud with sub-bottom profilers.

The search was not an easy one . . . but there, at last, was
the elusive *Mary Rose* once again.

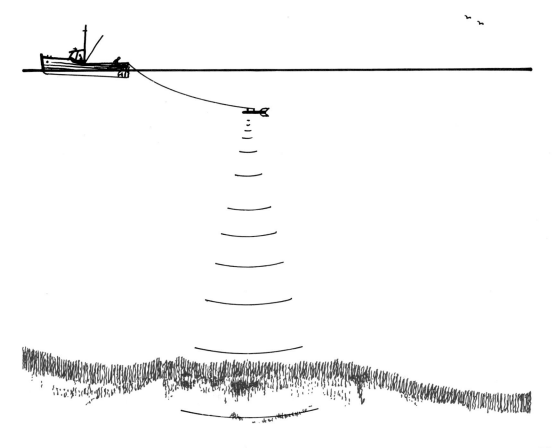

The underwater survey and excavation took from 1971 until 1982. Though so many divers and companies helped, it was an immense task to record and recover the contents of the ship, and prepare the hull for lifting. Since she was lying on her side, cut across by erosion, it was like trying to clear an enormous doll's house which had been shaken up, then filled with assorted muds and sliced through at 60 degrees. Some of the tools used would seem strange to a land-archaeologist (the air-lift shown in the drawing works like an underwater vacuum cleaner), but as on digs above the surface, skilled and careful hands rather than machines were needed for the delicate work.

Archaeology can be quite difficult enough on land
sometimes. Down in the cold and the filth on the bottom
of the Solent, it needs a particular kind of determination
to keep working dive after dive, day in and day out, with
the kind of conscientiousness that is necessary.

You are not down there for some quick grubbing after
'sunken treasure' – not just to find things and bring them
up. Shipwrecks are sometimes described as 'time capsules',
because with skilful excavation they can give a vivid
picture of how the people aboard lived. To capture that
picture, frozen in time at the moment of the tragedy, you
have to excavate and record meticulously, otherwise you
will destroy not just objects but information. You are
making an experiment that can never be repeated, digging
away mud that embeds fine layers of history. . . . It is not
just the object you find that is important, what matters
is how it relates to what is around it.

In the mud you have uncovered a box of surgeon's instruments.
Can you prove it is where it belongs in the ship? Or was it
thrown there as she heeled over? Did it get washed in much
later? Or fall when the timbers collapsed? Detective work
is needed at every stage, if the ship, and the life aboard
her, is to be reconstructed.

Down in the chill gloom, the position of every shred of
evidence had to be measured, plans drawn and photographs
taken. Over 17,000 finds were recorded, and when they were
brought to the surface, the work on them was only just
beginning. After 437 years under water, even the great
cannons, let alone things like an archer's quiver or a
sailor's hat, need special chemical conservation treatment
if they are not just to moulder away. Making them a durable
part of our maritime heritage will keep the laboratories
busy for years.

Nowadays, you do not have to be a diver to visit *Mary Rose*. Since 1982, the remains of her great hull have been safely ashore in Portsmouth. But even using modern salvage equipment, it did not prove easy to get her there. Henry VIII's Venetians were certainly not the last to find she was a difficult wreck to move.

By salvaging the 17th-century ship *Wasa*, in 1959, the Swedes had shown that it was possible to raise a very old wooden ship safely. Their experience proved valuable, and indeed the salvage ship *Sleipner* used by them also became 'mother ship' for the *Mary Rose* team. But in several ways, *Wasa* had presented an easier problem. She stood upright, on top of the sea-bed, with her hull basically strong and complete. She could be lifted in a cradle of cables, much as the Venetians had originally intended to do with *Mary Rose*. But not only was *Mary Rose* lying on her starboard side, deeply embedded in the mud – her missing port side meant that many of her remaining timbers had no support, and her whole structure might collapse if strain was put onto it unevenly.

To avoid this, once the hull had been emptied, hundreds of bolts were put into its strongest points, and from these wire ropes were passed up to a lifting frame, sitting on the sea-bed over the wreck on four legs, like a giant iron bedstead. From the archaeologists' measurements, an enormous cradle had been made to the shape of the ship. This was positioned on the sea-bed nearby, and padded with water-filled bolsters.

The idea was to use the frame to pick up *Mary Rose* very gently, spreading the strain through all the hundreds of bolts, and to lay her in the cradle. Then the whole assembly could be locked together, and lifted right out of the water with the ship in a safe sandwich of steel.

But there were problems. A 'bedstead' leg bent, so there was trouble in locking frame to cradle, and just as the giant floating crane *Tog Mor* was laying the 'sandwich' onto the barge that was to take it ashore, the frame slipped. But all ended well, and Prince Charles, the President of the Mary Rose Trust, who had often dived on the wreck, at last saw his ancestor's warship returning safely to her home port.

The remains of Mary Rose, *sandwiched between the damaged frame and the cradle, being lifted onto the barge on 11 October 1982*

A mill for grinding peppercorns: one of the extraordinary range of finds from the Mary Rose *'time capsule'*

The spur of a fighting cock, a surgeon's hat, lanterns and long-bows, gun carriages and galley pots, rigging blocks and rats' skeletons, gaming-boards and musical instruments; pikes, purses, parrels, pocket-sundials and pepper-mills . . . and all the other things, great and small, from a boatswain's whistle to the hull itself, were 'captured in the time capsule' the day the ship sank.

The story of the *Mary Rose* is by no means over. The rediscovery of the site, the patient work of the divers, the raising, and all the conservation efforts are really just preludes to the most intriguing part of all: working out what everything means.

A century and a half ago, interest in the cannons and other things brought up by the Deanes soon faded, because the historians of those days regarded them just as isolated objects, without much of a story to tell. Now, the *Mary Rose* archaeologists are studying their finds both individually and in relation to all those meticulous records of where each came from, in and around the wreck.

Over the years to come they will be able to reconstruct for us a vividly realistic picture not only of one of Henry VIII's leading warships, but of the lives as well as the deaths of those who went out aboard her to fight for England that bright Sunday morning in 1545.

INDEX

PHOTOGRAPHS   The photographs on pages 17, 29 and 30 are used by kind permission of The News, Portsmouth.

TITLE PAGE ILLUSTRATION   A gold coin recovered from the wreck, with the initials *H R* for Henricus Rex, 'Henry the King', flanking a crowned Tudor rose.

First published 1983   ISBN 0–7188–2587–X   All Rights Reserved

Typeset in Great Britain by
Nene Phototypesetters Ltd, Northampton

Printed in Hong Kong
by Colorcraft Ltd.